An Absolutely Candid and Insightful—While
Sometimes Humorous—Look at the Business World
as It Truly Exists and How to Move on the
CORPORATE ESCALATOR
WHILE ALWAYS GOING UP

None of Your Business

The modern day supervisor's Bible

WHAT YOU WILL NEVER LEARN, AND PEOPLE
WHO ALREADY KNOW WON'T TEACH YOU, IN
BUSINESS TODAY

By

David A. Trosper

authorHOUSE™

1663 LIBERTY DRIVE, SUITE 200
BLOOMINGTON, INDIANA 47403
(800) 839-8640
WWW.AUTHORHOUSE.COM

First published by AuthorHouse 09/13/04

ISBN: 1-4184-0000-9 (e)
ISBN: 1-4184-0001-7 (sc)

Printed in the United States of America
Bloomington, Indiana

This book is printed on acid-free paper.

None of Your Business is a truly realistic approach to the cutthroat life of business that employees and managers live every day. It is an easy read that can be finished in less than an hour but provides insights that will last a lifetime. Although many managers and upper managers in retail and business will find *None of Your Business* amusing, the amusement derives from the fact that they are looking at their supervisors and, at the end of the day, seeing themselves and their past failures as well. Whether you are an employee looking to get ahead or a manager looking to go further in your business, this book is a must-read to identify the pitfalls that keep people at a level of mediocrity throughout their entire careers. The teachings in the pages ahead will give you an insight like no other into business as it exists today and how you can break through to achieve unlimited success.

TABLE OF CONTENTS

ABOUT THE AUTHOR
DAVID A. TROSPER

Mr. Trosper has been involved with business at all levels for more than the past twenty years. He has held positions of upper management in numerous fortune 500 and fortune 100 companies. He has an uncanny understanding of business that comes from being a human lie detector trained in interviewing and interrogation.

Following time in the military he honed his people skills by receiving several degrees from institutes from California to Minnesota. He achieved a Masters of Arts in Theo centric

Business Ethics and holds numerous degrees in Business and Human Resources.

He is the owner of a national shopping and evaluation service used by retailers to test employee honesty and employee ethics. He has designed several tests used today by retailers to determine if an employee will remain loyal and honest and has conducted interviews with thousands upon thousands of employees for numerous corporations.

The beliefs in this book are not all shared whole heartily by Mr. Trosper but after studying how supervisors get ahead in business, they are what he proves to be the facts of the business world today and must be recognized by anyone wishing to get promoted.

Mr. Trosper provides coaching and training seminars to companies in the retail field to help management observe what to look for and how to motivate their associates to achieve goals and objectives.

The Jack Welch Way, The Sam Walton Story, The Henry Ford Story—these are just a few of the hundreds of books written about some of the greatest chief executive officers in our history of business in the world. There are also thousands of self-help books in print that will teach you how to achieve the success of these and other great chief executive officers. Read these books, and you too can become the CEO, the head honcho, the big cheese, the COO, and so on. Well, this book is totally different from any self-help management book you have seen or heard of. For every chairman of the board, CEO, COO, CFO, and president who helped author a great success story, there are millions upon millions of middle managers that **the teachings just do not apply to.**

Second, every self-help book authored or recommended by a great CEO in America will only affect great CEOs, not you or me. Now, here is the simple truth, but to some it is sadly a great shock. To get ahead in business today you cannot be honest and truthful all of the time. In fact, you must master the art of **BULLSHIT.** Some people call it tainting the truth, skirting the truth, flat out lying, as well as other things. You can call it what you will, but after I explain all aspects of business and how to achieve the highest level you can attain—or more important, the highest level you want to attain—then the bells and whistles will go off, and you will start to see the light. You see, contrary to the corporate mentality, it is not how hard you work that matters. It is more important how hard people above you perceive you are working. Is this fair? The answer is no—put quite simply, hell no, it's not fair—but you must get over it; this is business, and believe me, fair means nothing. Think about how many times in your life someone got promoted who did not work as hard as you or did not know as much as you. The answer for anyone who has spent time in business is many times.

That person knew the secret of how to convince the powers above that he or she should be perceived to be the right candidate for the job. If this person was not a qualified hard worker, then he or she was an expert at bullshit, tainting the truth, or flat out lying. Now, let's get to understanding the rules as they actually exist to get ahead in business and, more important, life.

Don't get me wrong; I believe in God, country, and well-being. But in business, you have to approach every opportunity as a failure or a success, and you must crush your opponent to win, and if you don't want to win, then you better get out of the game.

PEOPLE CAN SINK YOU
(Fire Bad Ones)

How many people do you know who should not be working for your company? I think if you really spent some time and evaluated this question and answered honestly, you would be surprised. In many situations in the corporate world, before we fire an employee, we make sure they do something wrong, and I mean very wrong. The employee has to violate a serious policy concerning ethics, steal from the company, or violate someone's civil rights—or worse, be on action plans forever and a day. We wait when the employee should have been fired years ago.

1

I remember taking over a division, and during the process of evaluating the employees, I was told about one employee who everyone said was a poor performer. When I went to his supervisor to find out about this employee, this is what I was told: "Yeah, he is really not a great employee, but he is a good guy and doesn't really do anything really wrong" (sound familiar?).

When I reviewed this employee's personal file, the last review he received was average.

It doesn't matter what your company does or how many people you supervise; this situation is bound to happen when you take over a department. So what do you do? In many self-help books, you will be advised on many ways to work with the employee to make him better, motivate him to succeed, lead him by example, and help him raise the bar. In some books, you may even be advised to let him go since he is your bottom 10 percent, and you need to upgrade your staff. Well, I guess all of these have a place in certain situations, but when you play to win, you must act accordingly.

The first thing to be done is what most people miss: Get rid of this person's supervisor. When you think about it, this supervisor is the one who let this employee continue at a pace that dragged the rest of the team down. If this supervisor is willing to let other departments see that your team has weak players, and it is accepted, then you are already on the path to failure.

If you are the new supervisor and have to address the problem, then this is how you get rid of it.

You have to remember that one of the most important things in business that you will ever learn is **KNOW HOW TO FIRE PEOPLE**. It is more important than knowing how to hire people.

First, take a partner, go to your human resources department, and use their knowledge and expertise. You must remember that in most cases human resources people are bleeding hearts. That's okay; that is why companies have them. Think about it, how can anyone who has the word *human* in his or her title not be warm and caring? With this in mind, in your first meeting with human resources, you never want to tell them you are going to fire someone. You want to tell them that you have a poor performer who is not meeting company standards. You want to put a plan together to let this employee know he is not performing to company standards and that you want to help him succeed. In fact, you should have a thirty-to-ninety-day plan to share with human resources on how you are going to do this. Once this is done, schedule a one-on-one with the employee. (And, by the way, make sure you have written the plan in such a way that the employee has no way of ever succeeding.) This may seem wrong, but if he improves enough to achieve the plan, you will be writing another one in six months, or worse, you will now have an employee who is just average at best.

Think about it, how many times have you had to write an improvement plan for your superstars? NEVER.

Sit down with the employee that you are going to fire. You notice I said "fire," not "give an opportunity to improve." Be honest with the employee, or better yet, have the employee perceive you are being honest. Let the employee know he is not what the company is looking for. Never make it personal; always blame the company.

Give the employee the plan and let him know the company is not going to let him succeed. Let him know you are on his side, and if he would like to resign, you would go to bat for him for a thirty-to-ninety-day severance. When you think about it, when an employee is no good, you're better off paying him to leave than monitoring his failures for ninety days.

In a worst-case scenario, if the associate becomes upset and complains, he now blames the company and not you,

Do I care more about the feelings of an under-performing employee than about me? If the answer is yes then work for a caring company like Enron, World Com, and many other companies.

You see, the point is that companies do not care. Some may try to appear as though they care, but this is only to win public sentiment to increase profits. If a public company cares more about people than profits, would anyone buy their stock? The answer is NO. They would then be a nonprofit company, and not because they intended to be.

PEOPLE CAN MAKE YOU
(Reward Good Ones)

Just as you must terminate your bad employees, you must also reward your good employees. You have to identify your superstars and make sure they continue to grow and make you look good. You very simply can do this by finding out what they appreciate the most and rewarding them with it.

Many supervisors will tell you that they have a certain group of people with basically the same pay range so they cannot reward the top performers effectively. If you are a supervisor who thinks this way, watch out, you may already be on someone's list to help you with your ninety-day plan.

If you have a 5 percent salary pool for ten employees, give it all to your top three performers. Let the other seven know what the company did. They will take it personally, and if they don't, then you know they are not in line for the next step. They will either rise to superstar status or move on. Either one of these choices gives you what you need to look good.

You must also remember that money is a great motivator, but there are many ways to motivate in and out of the budget. Look at it this way: If someone does something for you at your home, like the housecleaner or the gardener, you pay him or her, right? Of course you do. You pay him or her because he or she performed a service for you that you did not want to do or, more likely, what he or she did was not as valuable to you as your time if you had done it yourself. This is very simple logic that most people do not carry over to the workplace.

I remember one supervisor who could not give her top employees a bonus since the company was not doing well. She then told her staff that she was going to give three hundred dollars a month of her car allowance to the top three employees for the next six months.

She went on to say that she wished she could do more, and then set components on how to measure who the top three were. Her staff was so motivated by the gesture that her area performed at the top of the company and exceeded everyone's expectations. They not only made her look good, but they also worked so hard that she had to do 20–30 percent less work herself.

I found out later that this enabled her to spend less time at work, and she got rid of a $300-a-month housekeeper and did the housework herself. She then used the $300 she gave the top performers as a tax write-off. She was then given a bonus at the end of the year that far exceeded the amount she gave out anyway.

The reward can be a day off, lunch with a high-ranking official, casual dress, or so many more. The actual reward is not the key; the key is to get every one of your associates to strive to achieve greatness to be one of your top performers. You must start each and every day with the following two thoughts:

#1 Who are my top performers, and how can I reward them?

#2 Who are my bottom performers, and why have I not rewarded another company with them?

When you approach your staff in this way, you will be on your way.

KNOWLEDGE IS POWER
(Know the Answer, or Be Able
to Make Up a Good One)

Do you know your job and your company? GOOD as they

say in today's world that and a quarter, or should I say

$5 wouldn't even get you a cup of coffee in today's hard

world. First and most important! you need to know your

boss. Having knowledge about who your boss really is and

what he or she likes or doesn't like will mean more to your

career than knowing your company. I know what you are

thinking; I need to become a kiss-ass. No, that is not what

I am saying, but how many times have you said to your

counterparts, "The only reason that person got promoted is because he is a kiss-ass"? I want you to think about it this way.

When you were in college and the instructor in history said, "Forty percent of your grade will be based on your midterm test on American presidents," did you immediately say to yourself, "I am not going to kiss that instructor's ass and learn about American presidents"? The answer is "HELL NO." You crammed day and night for the next week to learn everything you could that might possibly be on the exam on American presidents. You did this for one reason: You wanted to pass and graduate from college so you could go on to your career and make big bucks. Well, your boss and your boss's boss are the American presidents, and you will need to always be cramming to learn everything you can about them so you can pass the exam.

(Remember, to fill your wallet with American presidents, you must learn everything about American presidents.)

You must first work on differing yourself from looking like a kiss-ass, as we discussed earlier. You must remember that in your boss's eyes there is a big difference between being perceived as a kiss-ass and being perceived as the person who your boss has gotten to know and feels he or she can depend on and trust to get the job done when it is needed. Remember, the old saying is true: "PERCEPTION IS INDEED REALITY."

For any of you who still do not get it, look at it this way. When you go out with someone on a date, do you go out and not try to find out what you can about the person you are dating? Don't get me wrong; I don't want you to look at your boss and think, "How can I get him or her in bed at the end of the day" (although this has led to some pretty great promotions). The only thing I want you to do is change your thought process and approach learning about your boss in the same way you already know how to learn about people in other situations.

15

I remember once I had a boss who very few people in the department knew much about since he was very guarded when it came to private matters. I called his wife and told her who I was and that the department wanted to get him a Christmas present, and we wanted to make sure it was something he liked. I learned more from talking to his wife for fifteen minutes about his personal life than anyone who worked with him for two years. I then gave him a handmade fishing fly from a small shop on the East Coast since his wife said he loved to fly fish.

The department gave him the gift, but I went a step further; I read up on fly fishing (my research on American presidents). You see, I did not know a thing about fly fishing, but my boss loved it, so I learned a little about it, and he called me more often, and we talked about fly fishing and then about work. You see, sometimes you may have the greatest ideas in the world, but if no one listens to them, you will be perceived as not having any ideas. You may ask if this got me a promotion. The answer is no, but when the company went through some tough times and was downsizing, three people were let go in my department, and I was kept. I have no doubt that when my boss had to make the decision to lay off three people, the feeling that he knew me personally had a great impact on my being kept.

Not only do you want to find out what your boss likes, but it is as important to find out exactly what your boss does not like and avoid it. I had a boss who had a conference call every Monday at 1:00 PM. It would make him furious if someone were as much as one minute late. Yet, still, for one reason or another, every week someone was late.

Find out what your boss likes and learn about it; find out what he hates and avoid it. Or more important, make your boss perceive that what is important to him or her is important to you as well. Remember, you do not have to like your boss. In fact, you may some day stab him or her in the back and take his or her job. But to stab someone in

17

the back, you have to get very close to that person and have him or her feel like he or she can trust you. So either way, make sure you know your boss. This way, you will be able to get close enough to stab him or her in the back, or just as important, you will see the knife coming when he or she goes to stab you in the back.

DON'T BE A FAT SLOB
(Image is Everthing)

I hope the title of this chapter got your attention; it was meant to. I remember a cartoon showing a fat, short, balding man who was very bright and dedicated to his company. This man was passed over for a promotion, and he went to his supervisor to find out why he was passed over again. His boss presented a tall, slender, good-looking man with perfect hair and said to the man, "This is Stan. We promoted him since he is tall and has executive-style hair." Believe it or not, this cartoon holds all too true in corporate America.

Don't get me wrong; I am not saying that a man who is obese or does not groom properly cannot get promoted. I am sure companies that make clothing for the big and tall are looking for people. As for the rest of the millions of companies out there, it does make a difference.

You must remember that every time a promotion is available, several people will be competing for the position. If it comes down to equal or close-to-equal talents, then the person who looks better will be given the promotion. Is this fair? HELL NO, but get over it; as we discussed, business is not fair. I had a person work for me for several years. He was the hardest working and most dedicated worker that I ever had, and he cared about the company. When I was promoted and moved on to another area, I recommended this person for my job. He was passed over for one reason: He was fat. The VP that made the decision felt that if he did not have the self-discipline to take care of himself, then how could he take care of an entire department? One does not have anything to do with the other, but the perception was one that this person could not get over. You must do your best to take care of yourself, both mentally and physically. Plus, you get an added benefit: You will probably live a longer and healthier life.

I am sure you have heard the old saying, "Clothes make the man." Well, there must be something to it, as an entire business has been built selling the fact that the right suit will get you ahead in life. When it comes to clothes, you do not have to be cutting-edge, but you do want to be professional and portray leadership in the way you dress. Just like physical features can sink you, so can the wrong attire.

I remember a female supervisor who was thought of very highly until one particular incident. She gave a presentation to a group of executives, and she wore a very tight-fitting, light-colored outfit with black undergarments. When she finished her presentation, one of the senior executives whispered to the rest of us, "We should have gotten her a pole to help her with her presentation," referring to what a stripper uses on stage.

What was lost in this was a quality presentation, and this image is now something that this person will have a hard time recovering from. You see, due to one presentation in the wrong clothes, she was now perceived to be a whore, and whether it is the furthest thing from the truth or not, we already know what perception is.

WHAT YOU NEED TO LEARN
(You Probably Already Know)

I have read—and more important, have been given—more self-help management books in my career than I can imagine. It seems like every supervisor I have ever had wanted to share with me the theory and the book it came from on how he became the great supervisor that he is. Well, the bottom line is simple: He convinced someone above him that he was the right person for the job. He was perceived as the right candidate for the job, and his supervisor probably gave him a book as well.

If I tried to live out the theory in every book, I would have gone from good to great, lost all the habits of unsuccessful people and learned all the habits of the successful ones, found the cheese, learned the Zen of modern management, been a one-minute manager, and so many more. Don't get me wrong; you can gain an advantage from a self-help management book in one instance, and here it is. If you read a few pages of a self-help management book that your supervisor gives you, then you can convince your supervisor that he or she was oh so wise, and you will now be a better employee.

The problem with these books is that they do not change the way you are. They can give you a good feeling of what you should be doing in business from the author's standpoint, but they will not result in a long-term fix. The reason for this is simple: Your next boss may disagree with your past boss's book, then you have lost the cheese and may starve without it, learned the Zen but have no one to Zen it on, or become a one-minute manager when your new boss wants an hour manager.

As the chapter says, you already know what you need to know; you just need to fine-tune your own skills, not live the way of one of these authors. What I mean by this is very simple. Get out a pen and paper and sit down, as I am actually going to recommend a self-help management book that a past boss gave to me. It was the only book I read that actually deals with business today and actually made some sense.

It was *All I Really Need to Know I Learned in Kindergarten*. It talked about very simple things, things such as share and play nice. I really don't remember the details of the book, but I think we can all relate to kindergarten. Think about kindergarten the next time you're in a boring planning meeting that seems to go on forever, as all of them do.

Don't wet your pants, don't eat dirt, and don't call your boss a poo poo head, no matter how much the last one fits. My point in all of this madness is very simple. Even the book that detailed how to succeed in business by relating to kindergarten really does not fit; do you really think sharing your great ideas will help you get ahead? If you do, then you better hope the person you share them with believes the same thing, or he or she will take your great idea and get a promotion using it as his or her own. As you can see, I really don't believe this book will help you in business, but it did have a catchy title.

The bottom line is that you probably know what it takes to succeed, so work on enhancing what you know, not what someone perceives you should know. Just remember to have your boss always perceive that you want to learn what he or she already knows.

Take your top five strengths that you know you have and learn how to make them even better. Or, even as, if not more, important: how to make top management notice your

strengths even more.

WORK SMARTER
(Not Harder)

Think about how many hours a week you work, and I do not want to hear the standard bullshit answer, "I work as much as it takes to get the job done."

#1 Write down how many hours a week you work.

#2 Now, write down how many hours a week you think you need to work to get promoted to the next level.

If number two is more than number one, very simply put, you have failed.

Remember this: The only time you want to work more hours is if you are getting paid by the hour. If you do not think this way, then by working more hours for the same pay, you are showing upper management that you are worth less than you actually are. The bottom line is that you are not smarter; you are dumber.

The reason behind this is that if you have to work harder to achieve the same results as someone working less, then you would not be a candidate for a promotion. The thinking behind this is that you would fail at the next level due to the fact you would have more responsibility and more work, and there wouldn't be enough hours in a day for you to succeed.

Do not get me wrong; you do not want to be perceived as lazy and always screwing off or leaving every Friday at noon. You have to learn to walk the thin line of appearing to work hard while not appearing to be lazy. You can be lazy; you just cannot be perceived as such.

A smart businessperson will tell you that in the world of corporate America the most important thing is to never miss a deadline.

Part of this is true. If you want to stall your career very quickly, then go into a meeting with a presentation that is not finished. The other part that is as important, if not more so, is to never look frazzled to make the deadline.

I remember a group of district managers who were giving presentations on profit margins. One of them got up in front of the group and shut down the overhead, had the lights turned up, and said, "Margins are what we're here to talk about, but how those margins affect people in this company has been overlooked." He then asked some key questions of accounting, production, and upper management of what they thought about the margin projections. After he had their answers, he went on with a presentation tailored to what they had said.

The bottom line was that he did not have a presentation, and instead of saying so, he let the people in the room with the answers do the presentation, and he looked like a genius in doing so. Remember, you do not have to know the answer; you just have to be perceived as knowing.

I remember once I was given a project to complete, and a supervisor in another area was doing the same project. (Remember, if you and a counterpart are given the same assignment, it is a test, and you are being thought of as a possible candidate for promotion.) I worked very hard and stayed late every day to complete the project. My boss would leave and say something like, "Burning the midnight oil?" I would reply, "Yes, whatever it takes," and continue working. My counterpart would leave with everyone else at 5:00 PM and say the project was going fine. When it came time to present our finished projects, they were almost exactly the same. Three months later, a promotion was available, and I knew it would be me. Everyone saw how hard I worked and knew I would do whatever it took to get the job done. Yet I was not given the promotion; my counterpart was.

The reason I was given for his getting the promotion was very simple. He had completed the project just as I had, and for him, it came naturally and was done during regular working hours. Upper management felt that since I had to work so hard and long that I would be overwhelmed at the next level, thus he was thought to be the smarter and more qualified for the promotion out of the two of us.

I found out about a year later that he had worked until 2 AM every day at home to complete the project and barely got it done on time. He just did not appear to have done it this way. Upper management's perception was that it came easy to him.

You may then ask how he was able to handle the overwhelming workload and responsibility of the next level. Just fine because perception works both ways.

As you climb the corporate ladder, you do not have to work harder. In fact, you work a lot less; you just get paid a hell of a lot more. You are just perceived to be working harder by people below you.

CRUSH YOUR OPPONENT
(There Are Winners and Losers in Every Promotion)

For every promotion in a company that you are striving to achieve, there will be several other people striving for the same promotion. This does not even include the outside candidates that will be considered.

Think about the last ten promotions from lower to middle management in your company. Chances are very good that up to half of them were filled by outside candidates. Many people ponder why this happens. The answer is simple: When it comes to outside candidates, all they have to do is be perceived in an interview as the person who can do the job. They bring no weaknesses to the position that are known.

The problem is that sometimes when you work for a company for an extended period of time, no matter how hard you work or how well you do, someone will remember a time when you screwed up. Then, when you are up for a promotion, someone brings it up, either directly to you or to the people responsible for making the decision. The only way you can offset this is by outweighing any screw ups with an abundance of good things you are known for doing within the company. If your company promotes 70 percent or even higher from the outside, this should tell you something. You probably need to leave to get promoted.

If your company promotes from within or you want to be part of that 30 percent that does get promoted, you need to start immediately and maximize the perception of your strengths while minimizing the perception of your weaknesses.

You do this very simply by strengthening your base for your strengths. When a new committee comes up or a project is looking for volunteers only, do it if it is one of your five strengths you identified earlier.

If it is not a strength, then you will not be impressing people, and you will probably be hurting your chances of promotion down the road, no matter how many extra committees you are on. If something comes up that you are not good at, you are better off getting out of it than doing it and showing everyone how inept you are. If they never see your weaknesses, then you look better and better, just like an outside candidate with no weaknesses, only better. You already know the company and can hit the ground running.

You see, when an outside candidate interviews, he or she will never tell a potential employer he or she has a weakness. Even if you look at the interviews that have been designed to get to this, you will not hear it in an interview. Think about it; if you were interviewing and asked someone, "What is your biggest weakness?" no one in his or her right mind would say, "I suck at public speaking," even if that were true. We have all been taught to turn this question into a positive by saying something like, "I am a little too much of a perfectionist, and I always go the extra mile to make sure everything I do is 120 percent when I complete a project, using an exorbitant amount of my free time," or some other bullshit canned answer. I am sure you are wondering why, if we all know the canned answers, we keep asking the question. Well, my friends, that is a subject for another book.

The bottom line is that you have to be perceived as not only being as good as an outside candidate but better, as you will always have some baggage. But if you have been paying attention, you will have several executives who perceive you to be the strongest candidate for the job, and then and

only then will you get the promotion every time.

NETWORK, NETWORK, NETWORK
(And Network)

In the old days, the ones prior to the '70s, people tended to stay at one company for an entire career. The security and benefits seemed to keep people from even tempting fate and looking for a new job. Also, the job search was done with a newspaper and/or a recruiter. People made a decent living and seemed secure with the company they worked for.

I remember a friend of mine—he wasn't really a friend but perceived me to be one—told me a story about his grandfather. His grandfather was a very bright software engineer and had worked at the same company for thirty-five years. Even though he probably could have made a lot more money and was even recruited to head up a new division of a start-up computer software company, he stayed where he was. He felt secure where he was; it was a Fortune 500 company and even boasted at that time that in fifty years they had not laid off an employee.

I think you can figure out the company I am talking about. In the last ten years, they have laid off employees in the tens of thousands and have outsourced jobs to foreign companies.

If you look at promotions to upper and senior management, then at least half come from the outside. When you are considered for a promotion, and it comes from the outside, do not take it personally. Look at it as an opportunity, as there is now an opening at the company the person came from.

The days of being loyal and dedicated to your company are far gone. If you think you should put your company first, then you need to think again. In today's cutthroat business world, you can be eliminated tomorrow to increase stockholder value so your company hits Wall Street's estimates.

If you want 100 percent loyalty, then buy a golden retriever. If you want loyalty in the workplace, then bring your golden retriever with you to work—I hear Petco allows them to come to the office—because that is the only way you will get loyalty at the office.

My point is very simple: Unless you are perceived as valuable by several different areas of the company, when the ax comes, you will go. This is why networking your strengths with several different areas of the company is so important.

Second and often overlooked is that you need to always network outside your company. Once I had a salesman who worked for me and always had the most contacts in business in any city that he worked in. It did not matter what the business was; when we needed something, he knew who to go to. Everyone perceived him as one of the hardest-working people out there, as he must have been out making contacts day and night. I found out he only worked an hour or so a day on the road and then worked a couple of hours networking from home. How he found the people to network was simple.

He went to the cities' office supply stores, and as you walk in, they have a briefcase that says, "Win this briefcase; drop in your business card, and we will draw a winner monthly." He would hit a few of these stores and take the cards. Shazam!—that was his network. He always left his card in the case when he took the others, figuring he would have a better chance of winning the briefcase. You see, perception with this person, as usual, was reality to the company. (You can also get the cards from restaurants that have a fish bowl to win a free lunch.)

The bottom line is that the more people you know, the better off you will be when you want a promotion, or the better off you will be when you need a job. Think of your job this way. When a new political party takes office, the cabinet positions are all replaced. The new people are the ones the leader has networked with to win the election. It does not matter how good the former person was, he or she is not aligned with the new administration.

You must always take time to seek out networking areas outside of work so you can always be on the inside. Talk with other people in your field regularly. Network with the local chamber of commerce, join business associations, and meet with the mayor, senator, governor, etc. You see, the more people you know, the better chance someone will know or recommend you for a job when you need one. And maybe more important, the better you are connected in the business world, the better chance you have of not having to look for a job, as you will be perceived as too valuable to let go in the first place.

I remember once I was offered a job by a company, and I decided to turn the position down. I did ask why they had sought me out for the position. They informed me that they were opening stores in a state where I had a personal relationship with the governor. I asked how they knew, and they said that one of their clients had seen my award on my wall. You see, I only met the governor once, and it was at some business symposium from which everyone got a letter for attending. I had framed the letter and placed it on the wall since it was signed by the governor and thanked me for the work. You always have to remember that what may seem like an insignificant contact to you may be the biggest one you need later.

The networking process should always be a part of your weekly activities. You can always network, and all too often, people overlook the places that can land them a job as they are going about their jobs or everyday lives.

Places to network are endless—your kid's school, the car dealer, the bank, the dry cleaners, city functions, county government, and so many more. You can even network while you are working. Think about the last time you traveled. You can reach out to attempt to network on the plane, at the hotel, on the rental car bus, and so on and so on.

I will never forget when the company I worked for lost a leading salesman to a rival. Everyone assumed he had been stolen away, and I found out later it had just so happened he had shared a cab with a senior executive of this company and, not knowing who the person was, networked and was later offered a job.

The bottom line is that, when in business, we all need to understand that everyone we meet may be a possible business contact, and we need to network accordingly. Keeping this in the front of your mind can only lead to positive experiences down the road.

FULLY UNDERSTAND THE PROMOTION
(Why Do You Want It?)

Why do you want to get promoted? This sounds like a stupid question, right? WRONG. So many times in life people strive to get promoted, and then when it finally happens, they are in awe, and the rewards are not what they thought they would be.

I remember moving my wife and two kids across the country from the West Coast to the East Coast for a promotion. I had absolutely worked my ass off—or I should say I had been perceived to have worked my ass off—for the promotion and was thrilled when it was offered. Once I got to my new location and had to start my life as well as my family's life over in a new and totally different culture, it dawned on me what a fool I was.

For a 10 percent raise and a title, I gave up a hell of a lot, and more important, my family had to give up a hell of a lot more. Even though they supported me and were proud, it was a huge mistake, and it becomes hard to shine at a new position when your family is miserable. Also, you need to remember that many of the people you will be supervising at first want you to fail, as some of them were probably in the running for the position.

In this case, I didn't stop there, and I built a quality team and was perceived to be a rising superstar within the company. Within two years, I was promoted again, and that was what I was working for in the first place. I say this because you have to know up front why you will take a promotion and exactly how far you will go to get it. Sometimes you must look at the position, and it doesn't take a genius to figure out why over 90 percent of senior managers in business today have been divorced. They got promoted by their company and got fired by their spouse. You need to know up front which is more important to you.

As the old saying goes, "You need to be careful what you wish for." I do believe that the promotion is what you were looking for and will work out if you approach it knowing in advance why you want it and what you are willing to go through for it. You just have to realize that you will have to give up things to get things. It may be friends or an area of the country that you want to live in, or in many cases, it could cost you your marriage.

If you have kids, you must realize that moving them at certain ages can screw them up emotionally for a long time. How many times have you seen very powerful people whose kids are screwed up? Many, I am sure. In closing, if you weigh the pros and cons, and you know the answer to

51

why you want the promotion, you will be starting off on the right foot when you get it.

WHEN YOU GET THE PROMOTION
(How Do You Keep It?)

When you finally get the promotion you have tried so hard to achieve, you must understand that in many cases keeping it can be just as hard, and sometimes harder. As I said earlier, as you rise up through the ranks, you won't have to work as hard because the higher you get, the less you work, but you will have to work smarter. You will now have to become, or at least be perceived as, a leader.

When you think of great leaders, who comes to mind? John F. Kennedy, Abraham Lincoln, Martin Luther King, and so on and so on. Well, some of the greatest leaders probably don't even come to mind, like Jim Jones and Charles Manson. "What?" you say. Don't get me wrong; these two are completely despicable people, and they deserve to rot in hell for eternity. However, think about their leadership skills. Manson had people kill for him without even batting an eye. Jones had people follow him across the world, and hundreds killed themselves at his command. Although the world of business will not come to this extreme, the saying is true: "Ultimate power has the power to corrupt ultimately."

With this being said, good or bad leaders were followed without question, and you can't even get a department to complete a budget, or even work as a team, so what—or more important, how—do you do it?

I think you need to turn to the greatest leader in history and follow the model he set down, and you will have no problems succeeding. The greatest leader ever in business was Jesus

Christ. Think about your business plan and follow me as I lay out his. I think if you look at what he accomplished—as he had a plan and was willing to do anything to achieve it—you will have your leader to emulate. You will just have to remember to tailor it to the cutthroat life that is business today.

#1 He had a plan.

#2 He rallied common people to carry out his plan.

#3 He always believed he was right, no matter what.

#4 He understood what the common person was all about and how to motivate him or her.

#5 He educated people on how they could make a difference.

#6 He put together a group of top advisors (disciples).

#7 He had a man at the top he could count on; it helps when your dad is GOD.

#8 When things seemed hopeless around him, no matter what, he was the calming influence.

#9 Toward the end, he never thought about himself.

And last but not least

#10 HE WON.

Use this logic to set your goals as a leader, and I guarantee you will succeed.

And remember, even Jesus was stabbed in the back by one of his top advisors for silver. When you always remember this, it won't be so tough to always believe a coworker will stab you in the back for your promotion.

ABSORB THE BODY BLOWS
(But Protect the Chin)

Since we ended the last chapter with Jesus, we will start this chapter with an analogy of him as well. When people think of why Jesus died on the cross, they come up with numerous theories. But the simple truth is that his power was feared by the people who crucified him. Now, obviously, you as a supervisor will not be compared with Jesus, and you will not be crucified. Be careful of the last thought, as in business I have seen numerous times a group of employees banded together and had their supervisor crucified, or, as we call it in business, fired.

You see, when you get promoted and are working in a supervisory capacity, not only are the stakes higher, but the treachery becomes higher as well.

If you think of some of the greatest boxers of all time, what do you think of? A great hook, great jab, great upper cut? Well, these are all important, but if you ask any great boxer, he will tell you that you have to be able to take a punch.

When you look at a fighter, you will notice that he keeps his hands high, because one fatal blow to the head can end the fight. What he leaves open is the body, because he knows he is in condition to absorb body blows. More important, while his opponent is throwing body blows, he is tiring, leaving himself open for a solid punch to the head that can end the fight.

When you work with a group of fellow supervisors, you all work as a team for the common good of the company. If you believe this, you have not been paying attention. This statement is heard at many companies and is pure crap. If this were actually true, then why would companies put goals out such as sales leader, margin leader, and so on and so on, making winners and losers in every area of the company?

Now, your boss may want his team to work together to create great ideas for the good of the company, or should I say for the good of him or her, so he or she can shine.

Do you think in a cutthroat environment where, say, the winner in sales gets a cruise, the person with the answer is going to share it with you for the common good of the company? HELL NO. So, what do you do? Very simply, you share the small wins so everybody on your team believes you are a team player. Once you have achieved this, when the time is right, you throw the head blow and WIN, WIN, WIN with the big ideas.

You see, in the end, you are a winner if not only you think you are but in business if everyone above you perceives you are.

Now, go out there and become the supervisor that every company wants to hire, and one that your company will do anything to keep. You see, when it's all said and done, YOU AND ONLY YOU have the ability to make people perceive whatever you want; therefore, regardless of education, background, or knowledge, you can rise to any level you wish.

DEDICATION

I dedicate this book to my loving wife, Lynne. Regardless of having to live with me for the past twenty years, she has always been a light in a sea of fog. With the business world that I work in being what it is, she has always striven to see the good in people and believes to this day that people can make a difference in business as well as life.

It is because of her I continue to grow and move forward in life.

(Or at least I am perceived to be doing so; only I know for sure.)

To book Mr. Trosper for motivational speaking engagements or to have him provide one-on-one counseling for your company as he has done for so many in the past, he can be contacted at:

American Retail Resources

2416 Woodridge Road

Fort Mill, SC 29715

AmericanRetail@AOL.COM

www.ingramcontent.com/pod-product-compliance
Lightning Source LLC
Chambersburg PA
CBHW022131170526
45157CB00004B/1838